STITCHED ON ME

Hilary King

Riot in Your Throat
publishing fierce, feminist poetry

King, Hilary.
1st edition.
ISBN: 979-8-9889898-3-7

Cover Art: Bailey Pfohl
Cover Design: Kirsten Birst
Book Design: Shanna Compton
Author Photo: Hilary King

Riot in Your Throat
Arlington, VA
www.riotinyourthroat.com

what we will become
waits in us like an ache.
　　　　　—Lucille Clifton

CONTENTS

THE DOG WAKES ME UP IN THE MIDDLE OF THE NIGHT

Come see the moon, she says. So I go. The backyard is quiet and dark, thick with shadows, the grass clipped, the roses overgrown. The dog nudges me with her nose. You're drinking too much, she says, her eyes locked on mine, her long tail wagging. It's getting sloppy, she adds. She's a purebred. She was expensive, but I wanted children and I wanted dogs and one was allergic to the other. Wants can be managed, though. My dog says, You need to cut down. Get yourself back to normal. I shrug. I look up and realize I don't actually see the moon.

STITCHED ON ME

Here we women root ourselves
in the humid soil of expectation.
Deference our genus.
Watch us bend towards each other.
 You're prettier.
  You're smarter.
 I'll clean the kitchen.
  You run the war.

To shout
 I want.
To whisper
 I won't

My mother stitched on me
the monogram of martyrdom,
the blood she drew matched
what she'd worn all her life.

What a clean kitchen I have.

MY CLOSET

Like a disco in some 1980s Eastern Bloc country. So many stripes. So many wide-legged pants. The sequined dreams of a trapped people. Sweaters pilling like acne-faced teenagers. Ballet flats and riding boots. Each set of heels seems to have one shoe with a broken strap. Why? What happened? A hook holds a cluster of tiny sparkly purses with straps long as reins, the insides of which are littered with ancient cigarettes, orangey lipsticks, and despair. The door here won't close all the way.

PANTOUM WITH ENVY AND EMILY DICKINSON

This feather in my chest.
How did it get stuck there,
who buried the key?
Don't say me, Emily D.

I was looking up. I saw
who flies with the gods like
Mary O. and Emily D.,
their bones, their arrows.

Those who fly with the gods
try their wings out on the ground.
I let my bones get crumpled under
muddy envy and clayish compare.

I must learn to grow the wings
of beauty and other birds not born
of stone envy and childish despair.
What separates winged and walking?

Beauty and other idols not busy
measuring this feather in my chest.
What separates winged and slithering?
Don't say me, Emily D.

ROOMS AFTER A FUNERAL

Too young to hold or bless my mother's hands
as she wept into them, sitting next to my brother
as they both shook with grief, I moved like a breeze
through the forest of strangers crowding our house,
the place we'd moved to before cancer moved into my father.
That house my mother's shout, each room her echo,
fern wallpaper in the dining room, gingham
in my sister's room, the banister she polished back
to brightness. I fled from her silhouette that night
to the top of the house, to my mother's studio,
her easel square in the middle of the room,
anchor to the ship of her ambition.
She wouldn't sail again for years.

SELF-PORTRAIT AS ANNE SEXTON'S TYPEWRITER

Not upright and boxy as my predecessors,
I was lean and long and tan. I was modern.
I was her pet, wasn't I? It was me she loved,
me she wanted to be with first, later, last.
Not the husband, the lovers, the betrayers.
Interrupted from our hour by her daughter,
she flung me at that daughter. And Reader,
I leapt into mother's violence, my keys of steel
clacking, my carriage swinging, my ribbon spooling
to be back alone with my mistress, to be teased
by her nicotine-scented fingers. Don't pretend,
Writer, you haven't lifted your instrument, hefted
its weight in a clenched fist when another voice
calling your false name pierces the lovely, empty page.

COLOR ME BEAUTIFUL™

Winter, my mother was christened,
and she smiled, reborn in jewel tones.
Summer, my sister was crowned. Then,
the oracle tilted my chin and paused.

Spring, I think, said this woman, our neighbor
one block over. *She should wear pastels. Pinks.*
My mother gasped: *Like your Easter dress!*
I flinched. My sister smirked. At sixteen,

she knew how to starve desire, what to carry
in a purse, to never wear a too-tight pink dress
even at Easter, especially if your mother
makes you. I clutched my empty Bermuda bag.

I liked how the wooden handles felt,
how the covers hid the plain fabric,
how the covers could be changed,
how the emptiness there could be filled.

THE YEAR I WORE HEELS

It wasn't actually a year,
but it was more than twice.
I'd lost weight, covered
the darkest of my roots.
I wanted to try flying.
Oh, I wobbled, I tottered, I
clunked, clunked, clunked
down the long hall
of self-esteem.
Did I miss gravity's grip?
Yes, but from the top
of confidence
I could see
how everything got built.

STANDOFFISH

I never saw my mother hold her husband's hand
 or stroke his blue-blazered shoulder.
Compliments were reserved for thin women and
 handsome priests. London and her last
two houses brought brightness to her eyes.
 Her greatest affection she saved
for a succession of Scotties, a breed known to be aloof.
 Each one she fed into obesity,
half her plate scraped into the dog's pedestaled dish.
 Lamb chops, chicken, potatoes
au gratin. *What's wrong?* she'd ask, her face
 pinched when the dog turned up
its long whiskered nose. *What else can I give you,*
 she'd persist, her eyes wet, the dog's
unblinking. So stood love in my childhood, begging
 over an overflowing bowl.

HALF SLIP

This pretense of silk,
trimmed in lace,
lipped with elastic.
Champagne-colored layer
our mothers wore
to make their faces
hang straight.

IF MY 1970S CHILDHOOD HAD AN INSTAGRAM FEED

*". . . for teen girls who'd recently experienced body image
issues, Instagram made those feelings worse . . ."*

—The Wall Street Journal

Child body:
Age of elbows and knees,
pedaling, running,
finding home in grass and trees.
View how eras come to an end.

My sister:
Older, taller, residing already
in skirts and manners,
cursive ideas of womanhood.
See her dream to be a model, the headshots taken.

My brother:
Wit our family language,
cruelty our dialect,
he, the expert linguist.
Hear his nicknames for me: Porkbutt, Jellybowl, Fat Albert.

A man in a South Carolina gas station pointing
to a nine-year old girl's stomach
saying—
Find the lie when I say I can't remember exactly what he said.

Farrah Fawcett Poster:
Red swimsuit barely cupping
her breasts
yet loose on her waist.
Observe how I made a poster of that looseness and hung it on a wall in my mind.

My 13-year old body:
Mushrooming, seeping, flood
and fire every month, a jungle
in khakis and button-downs.
Hack at the vines sprouting everywhere.

My mother, her mother, all mothers:
Buttoning, straightening,
smoothing, pushing, reaching
down their daughter's throat.
Trying to strangle the future.

80s mall:
Hot tears, cold dressing room,
mannequins' pale stillness.
Victoria's Secret an alien planet.
Walk alone down to Lane Bryant.

Glossy bibles named beauty:
Brimming with confidence
how-tos in the front, six pages
of Kate Moss in the back.
Retch from binging advertising.

Skinny Jeans:
Low rise, slim fit.
How a thigh gap
became a mountain top.
Count the bodies that died on the climb.

My body my battlefield:
Dream of conquering.

Dream of surrendering.
Trace the skirmishes
in the lines around my eyes.

HER UNIFORM THEN

Her rainbow had one color: black. Not sexy, fishnet, or even goth black. The black of alone: walking alone, shopping alone, eating alone, sleeping alone, and crying. She knew she didn't look good. She knew she didn't know how to look good. Not then. She was all feelings then. Dark, unhappy, ill-fitting feelings. Everything she put on sagged or unraveled. Always a thread trailing down her hip or elbow. She didn't care. She couldn't. She was deep in it then, and this was the uniform. She proved a hard worker in this field.

CROP TOP

"[Rent the Runway] has seen four times the demand for crop tops in 2021 compared with 2019, including triple the demand from women 35 and older . . ."

—New York Times, May 25, 2021

This flesh, this muscle of us,
    maybe that's what kept our selves
together in this too-long echo,
    a ligament holding close
the bones of being mother, daughter, sister,
    teacher, boss, lover, keeper
of feeling, filler of days.
    We kicked up the sun.
We tucked in the moon.
    Nights we ran,
holding each other's hands.
    Now other hands are holding.
We can cast off our lessness,
    reveal, below the heart,
our own bare skin.

TARGET IS A BAR I GO TO SOMETIMES

where I get drunk on $10 T-shirts
and tassel necklaces. I flirt with throw pillows.
I pass out on washable indoor/outdoor rugs.
Like the second hand on a broken clock,

my molded plastic cart stutters through the store.
I'm the hours here, the minutes, the years.
My children stay small, wear sock feet forever.
We drink up the aisles together, days so delicious,

their needs and mine so simple, so easily
filled—a mug, vitamins, love that isn't
grudging. Sunlight in the parking lot
hangs on my shoulders like a lover.

HOW TO WEAR YOUR MOTHER

First touch, first pull of cloth
around small shoulders.

Should the mirror blind you.
    You look
    like
    a sack of potatoes.

Should the mirror's glass break.
    You'd be
    happier
    if you lost weight.

Sew your own adornments.
    That's cute.
    Where
    did you get that?

First sadness, and the last.
Every stitch between.

CROSSBODY

The day my 10-year-old daughter started taking Prozac,
I go full Baggallini. Cry-walk into my local gift shop,
stationery in the back, greeting cards up front,
in between bath salts, travel alarms, fuzzy socks.
This was my mother's store. Not mine. Not

yet. Please not yet the need for socks both fuzzy
and slip-proof. Couldn't I still trust where I tread
in the world? Until my daughter needed a pill
to push through her clouds, I kept my dreams loose,
tossed into whatever I carried with me every day.

I was ambitious and Christ my shoulder hurt, carrying
a bag full of notebooks, books, pens, lipstick,
another notebook, another book.
If an hour or an idea appeared, I was ready.
Now, therapists and teacher conferences later,

I wanted a separate pocket each for
grief, for anger, for courage.
What I needed to be ready for now
had to be packed precisely and worn throughout the body,
right across the heart.

LEATHER JACKET

I was black on the outside, red on the inside.
Sturdy, with deep pockets.
She liked me right away.

17-year-old girl on a year abroad,
found me in some tourist market, plucked me
from the crowd. Wore me home.

She kept her cigarettes in the inside pocket,
taking them out, tucking them back in,
as if it was her heart she kept putting away.

We were close, those wandering, shivering days.
It was me she pulled around her shoulders
the night things went too far. Pulled her hide on

and we got the hell out of there. She slept with me
beneath her cheek, woke with my scars.
She was red on the outside, black on the inside.

WHEN I WAS A KNIFE

Women gathered to me then,
admiring how I had
whittled myself
away.
How much did you lose?

I took their polish.
I shone.
You look great.

A knife doesn't know
how sharp its blade is
until the cuts begin.
Skinny fucking bitch.

LIPSTICK SOLDIERS

Battles they fought,
battles they won,
battles they lost.

My mother and her comrades,
in beauty's army until the bitter end,
present arms every morning.

Hallway mirror marching ground.
Heels planted, elbows up,
mouths in formation.

WHAT WOMEN WEAR FOR RESURRECTION

The first Easter dress a woman wears
floats with handsewn cherries or flowers,
the fabric blossoming out from her waist like a bell.
Everyone admires the girl child, imagines
how sweetly she'll ring someday.

The last Easter dress she wears for several Aprils running,
a tasteful floral with long sleeves because the church
is always cold, so cold she finally says to hell with it,
spends Sunday at the movies followed by Thai food,
the whole day in comfortable slacks she thanks God for.

Years between, the dress is straight, sleeveless,
solid-colored. A sheath, as in a loose covering
for a sword. By the end of this holiday of food,
family, and religion, a man has risen but a woman
wants to lie down and remove her own hot metal.

THE VOLCANOLOGIST

Another dry day, the sun unclouded in the 7am sky,
the dog's leash heavy and hot in my hand.
I thought the volcano would fix the weather,
my husband says and I realize

                     how wrong I've been,
how poorly I use the space we save for dreams.
His a meadow, a green and daisied place

where seeds of knowledge blow in, then
promptly blossom. He could become
a volcanologist yet, my husband thinks.

I've let sorrow fill the sky between my ribs,
become a spillway for all our floods:
daughter's bloody bitten nails, cancers,

accounts due. Who the better steward of
their acreage? Not the one squinting
and sweating, struggling
to pull the family
dog from the bushes.

THE UPDATED ENCYCLOPEDIA OF FEMALE PHILOSOPHERS

Books change people. Do people change books? My son used to gnaw the corners of his picture books until stories dripped down his chin. My mother arranges hers by color, like flowers in tall wooden vases. I lay out my books on my bed: mysteries, cookbooks, a farmer's almanac from the flood year, a field guide to trees, the updated encyclopedia of female philosophers. I lay them out in the shape of a middle-aged woman, then I lie on top of them and pray. How many books does it take to change a light bulb? None. We've memorized this darkness. I wake up with the corners of my personality folded down and my margins full of notes.

HOW MANY GOOD YEARS LEFT?

Ask the doctor,
the therapist,
the machines at the gym.
Interrogate insomnia.
Query ambition.
Question your next
glass of gin.
Study the statistics.
Review your genetics.
Ask your mother's face
when she lies, *One day
I'll be traveling again.*
Ask the shadow slanting
across your pen.

DRESSING IN MY FIFTIES

Gravity has lost its grip on me.
Each trip around the Sun
grants me greater propulsion.
To tether myself to Earth,
I must wear

this straw fedora,
these red high-top sneakers,
this quilted yellow jacket, this scarf
of orange flowers and bright blue fear,
a locket for each lost house,
a gemstone for each dream surrendered,
a watch telling time of my own invention.

MY HUSBAND ASKS ME IF I EVER THINK ABOUT RONALD REAGAN

I think of his wife, her hair as fixed
as her loyalty, her unhappiness

casting its humpbacked shadow. I think
of my own hair. Lately I've been proud

of my lawless curls, the years it took
to unstraighten myself.

I can never get the comb through
the strands at the base of my skull.

It's forever tangled there—pride, desire,
selfishness. I run my finger there,

measuring. No, I never think about Reagan,
I lie to my husband.

THERAPY OF RED VINES™

I don't sit in a minivan
at nine o'clock at night
in a CVS parking lot
eating Red Vines for pleasure,

I tell my imaginary therapist.
I'm eating my feelings.
Your feelings taste like
licorice? My therapist asks.

Yes, I say, this clichéd rage
goes down like a pound
of red gummy sticks that
threaten my teeth and

reduce my stomach
to rubble for days.
Therapy was my husband's
idea, one he would hand

to me when I was down
like a tissue or an apple.
I enjoy apples, how they sit
so solid in the hand, then

their flesh weighs less than
a whisper within the body.
Whispering works as well
as shouting, my pretend therapist says

but I can't hear anything
over the twisting of the empty
licorice wrapper as I
ball it up in my fist.

THREE SHADES OF BLUE

On the Goodwill rack,
three pairs of jeans. New.
Same brand, same size,
designer tags still
dangling on thin
black strings.

Someone dreamed
a dream in three
shades of blue.

It's a trick of light
the way oceans, mountains,
and happiness shine blue
from a distance.
Blue as the late-July sky, blue
as a high mountain lake,
as afternoon shadows on snow.

IF HUNGER IS A MASK, I AM NEVER NAKED

your face : sour candies in
a covered dish : another argument
resentment thickening in my mouth
your fist against the door : rolling
boil : wine and steak : whose sacrifice
when : the silence between us : bowl
of stone fruit : peel apple into apology
a cautionary tale : my spoon stabbing
ice cream in the freezer's yellow light

WHAT DAUGHTERS WEAR TO FLY

In airports all over the world,
girls are preparing to fly.
They travel without the armor
of their mothers. No overstuffed purse,
no jacket with familiar pockets,
no shoes appropriate for departing one place
and arriving in another. No, our daughters
wear T-shirts, leggings, flip-flops thin
as the heart of the patriarchy.
I'm not cold,
my daughter insists during the red-eye
and indeed she never shivers or stumbles
as she pulls our baggage behind her.

MAVERICK

Lately when I wake up in the middle of the night—
in my fifties, the Earth a wreck, the US worse—
I think about *Top Gun: Maverick.*
What was the mission of the flight unit?

I remember Jon Hamm's face, serious, slightly sweaty
as he stood in front of a map and explained the mission.
Something about a canyon and one chance to drop a bomb,
then fly up the other side of the canyon before the enemy arrived.

One chance, and very little time.
Katie Holmes hit her target. She needed a burner phone
and a secret apartment in New York but she left Tom Cruise
and divorced him in ten days. *Ten* days. A surgical strike.

Can I be that precise? That fearless and disciplined?
Fly out of this canyon of middle age, opportunities behind me,
steep cliff of aging parents and failing body before me,
my dreams a small red X in enemy territory?

I don't want to be Miles Teller, looking out the window
for the enemy until time arrives in an ominous shadow right above me.
This is why I'm like this, grinning, panicked, pulling stupid moves
that could get me killed or kicked out of everything I love.

I wanna be Maverick, Ray Bans and million-dollar smile.
I wanna hit that target, leave smoke rising behind me.

MY MOTHER EATING ONION DIP

Unroll a reverie.

Mother and daughter
eating onion dip,
discussing how
to park money offshore.

A mother's job
is teach her children
to secure funding,

to cut the dead weight.
Family is what matters,
my mother says,

and who
handles your taxes.
We clink our glasses.

The ice rattles.
Go ahead, she says,
pushing the bowl

of chips towards me.
I select a perfect oval chip
and lean

deep over the dip.
I feel her pride on me
like salt.

TRYING ON

I can't find parking at the store I need to go to, but the shop across the street
has open spaces. So I go in. The space is light and airy, the racks full but
not crowded, the lighting pleasantly warm on my face. I notice this place
sells everything I ever wanted to wear but never dared to: leopard-print
pants, crop tops, horizontally-striped A-line skirts, camping, small business
ownership, farming. Farming? Try it, the salesclerk says. She's dressed in
black, and her bangs are epic, like an old black and white photo of a library in
Dublin. I find myself in the dressing room trying on lambing and FSA loans.
Heavy boots. I lift my feet, try dancing. How's the fit, the saleswoman calls.
I can't tell if I'm swimming or drowning, I tell her. Do you have anything in
cafes or bookstores? Maybe a bakery? As she shakes her bangs no, an older
woman wearing a measuring tape around her neck and rows of silver bangles
up each arm approaches. Let's take in the acreage, she says quietly. Perhaps
remove the sheep but keep their idea. As she lays the tape against my waist,
her bracelets move without a sound.

LEARNING TO ACCELERATE

Downhill,
tuck your
elbows.
Loosen
your grip,
lean into
gravity.

Uphill,
knees pistoning,
calves bulging,
be surprised
how high
you can climb.

The wind's
your enemy
until turning
makes it
a friend.

What a relief
it is to be
the engine, to be not
the passenger
but the creator
of speed.

TWO MILLION SIT-UPS LATER

The way Ben's hand swept across JLo's ass,
    polishing her like a truck he'd just bought,
his skin smooth, his teeth spotlight white.
    The JLo back then wore newsboy caps and big hoops,
her eyes wide, her brows lifted as if fame
    was a surprise, as if she didn't know for what rewards
she crunched that stomach three hundred and twelve times a day.
    Two million sit-ups later, it's Jennifer who wears Ben,
wears him like a brand-new Birkin, handsome consolation
    for the Oscar not won, for being cheated on,
for the tabloid's fairy-tale-gone-wrong narrative.
    They look cute, Jen knows, in sweaters on Instagram,
and *girl* we agree. We heart emoji. We fire emoji.
    Is this reunion real?
Does love always become a negotiation?
    Shrug emoji. Eye roll emoji. Eggplant emoji.

SKIP THE SCARF

For Christmas don't give me jewelry or perfume.
I want a vending machine, I tell my family.
A food truck, a car wash, and also
a strip mall. I want an empire.

I want my daughter to want one too.
Be selfish sooner, I teach her.
Hunger for more than approval,
that cozy pink bathrobe you can't stop wearing.

Don't wait until no one is in front of you
to put yourself first. *I just want love,* my mother
would answer, *and perhaps some bubble bath.*
The bottles piled up. The tub waited for her
like a white porcelain grave.

EVERYTHING ABOUT MY BROKEN WRIST IS PRIVILEGED

How I broke it skateboarding
at age 54. How immediate
my treatment, how swift
the surgeon. How my insurance
covers two appointments a week
with a trained professional who turns
an extremity of my body
back and forth,
back and forth.
With oiled fingertips
she coaxes the scar tissue
away from the tendon,
trying to return my motion.
I feel like a queen.
She even stops when I grimace and whisper,
hurts. How I am able to ask myself
How much wrist do I need?
How I know the answer
doesn't hurt at all.

PELAGE

I wear a coat of scars,
marks striated and white,
broken clouds.

Collected by accident,
and by intention.
I did not dream of this

yet here are bits of myself
at twelve, eight, five
sewn into the lining
of how I wear the days.

EYELINER

Mornings my eyes thick
with the debris
of last night's dreaming.

I have to knife
color
out of the pencil.

Rough canvas, age.
What I want seems to be
narrowing.

Coffee, time,
the frame of being
myself.

LOOSE FITTING

To live in today's weather,
I wear my pockets filled,
blue linen, and a necklace
of yellow flowers.

Fashion says volume
should be balanced:
Tight on top, relaxed
below. Accentuate

the waist. Draw the gaze,
we're told, to where
we take up less space.
Today I moved like curtains

blowing, windows open,
a clean house in May,
my foundation not
settling but dancing.

THE WITCH EXPLAINS HERSELF TO SNOW WHITE

Don't be scared, Snow honey. I don't want
your beauty. Didn't I already have it?

Didn't I once wear my dress so low, my lips
so red? Didn't I once serve the house of little men?

I did, Snow honey, I did. For too long, far too long.
Years of scraping and bowing and pretending

the sound from my mouth was singing, not screaming.
I too waited for a prince to kiss his life into mine.

As if I didn't already have the forest, the trees, the shadows.
Who needs a prince when you have a basket of apples?

GINGER SPICE ONLY WEARS WHITE

The low-cut daring you slipped over your head
on Saturday nights. The expensive ambition
you zipped into every Monday morning.
They will lie someday among dust bunnies
in the far fields of your closet.

Even the boiled-wool, big-buttoned,
pockets-full-of-dandelions-and-tears
coat of motherhood will someday
sway from its own padded hanger.
What you wore in your 20s won't fit

your 40s. Saints don't begin with halos.
We gain, we lose, we acquiesce. Ginger Spice
only wears white now, her Union Jack corset days
swapped for farm life and cozy sweaters
in the color of clouds and baby lambs.

WIDE-LEG PANTS

Enter with the wind,
sails full.
Leave a wake
of yourself.

EDGESTITCH

First you were the thread. Now you are
the needle, easing your mother's arms
into her coat as she stands docile as a child.
Once you chafed in her grip, mornings
she combed out your wildness,
bleak seasons she harvested only your flaws.
In return you gave her silence.
It takes her slow unspooling
to weaken the knots between you.
When she trails off over lunch, staring
silently at her soup, you pick up the thread,
talking, telling, keeping the needle moving.

DIAGNOSIS WITH COMPOSITE ORGANISM

The doctor mutters my diagnosis, her mouth
fenced around the first word: *Lichen.*
    A tree falls, blocks my mind's path.
Lichen sclerosus, the doctor clarifies, *very common*
in post-menopausal women.
The whole forest falls over.

I picture women at the Y,
the older ones there every morning
lifting, running, sharpening themselves
into spears aimed at age. Behind them
careers, kids, marriages, so many pasts,
so many branches tangled.

Now, as they begin to revert
back to earth, something new grows,
something frilled, something strong,
on the inside of their wrist
or soft underside of breast, skin
pearling over stone.

MOTHER'S PURCHASE

Time hides in a new dish towel
dotted with sunflowers and pumpkins.
Your mother's past redacted.

The long wandering, the lunges at life.
Fingers that once flicked cigarettes
now sense when the blade's become

too dull to make a meal. She brings
the steel down anyway, splitting
one breast into two, three. Smaller

portions cook faster. Polluted hands
remember to reach for old rags. *Don't
use my new one,* she'll scold you later.

ETERNAL CHERRY, MAYBELLINE 24-HOUR SUPER STAY LIPSTICK NO. 200

What's eternal about cherries
except the dream
of a perfect red ripeness?
Elusive as a truly low-maintenance haircut,
jeans that fit,
glasses that flatter.

The best cherries I ever had
came from Walmart,
not red but maroon, not round
but a squished round-*ish.*
I ate them out of the bag,
their flesh meaty and sweet,
slightly zingy.

I bought this lipstick there too,
then again and again wherever
I could, bringing to an end
a search not for perfection,
but the better, a fruit I was certain
grew just beyond my reach.

MIDNIGHTS, MIDLIFE

Nothing in caliginosity trips me anymore.
I know where the floor slopes down. How
one chair at the table always gets left

bereft. I slip through rooms holding only
attention, the blackness too complete to sip
from a book or work the broom of ambition.

I pull silence around me like a sweater,
step past the waiting table with its bowl
of apples beginning to shrivel. I leave

the chair to its motherless loneliness.
At the long window, I watch the rats
come out of the ivy to do their work.

GRAY-HAIRED SYLVIA PLATH

Would have been a pain in the ass.
She would have written too much,
posted too much, spoken up, spoken
ill, been reviled, been adored, become
a gray-haired laurel-adorned bore.
Aging a lesson few teachers master
and no student remembers. I struggle
in my studies. Wisdom eludes me,
regrets still fill corners of my life.
She enjoyed weaving and keeping bees,
and she wrote her best poems last.
I pray I survive my own cold London
hells to do half as much half that best.
Sylvia Plath would have kicked ass.

WOMAN BECOMING WINSTON CHURCHILL

It happened after menopause. My waistline and my comfort with power grew imperceptibly until one day I found myself having whiskey at breakfast and convincing America to enter the war. Older women knew this would happen, but they didn't tell me. Politics. When you're young, you want to be lithe, diplomatic. You want to appease everyone. Now all I want to do is to crush the fucking Nazis. It's not just that I want to set the world right; it's that now I know how to. My new capability. I realize I'll end my days out of power, painting watercolors and writing memoirs no one will read, but not yet. Not yet.

BURY ME IN COASTAL GRANDMOTHER

*"The Coastal Grandmother aesthetic embraces lifestyle choices,
and leisurely walks on the beach are included."*

—Southern Living Magazine

Gone the bright colors that prop up midlife:
yellow hello, red armor.
Banished the leather jacket, the *screw you*
of school pickup years.
Good riddance to skinny jeans
and tiny dreams. What's left:
a meal, a drink, to sleep

through the night twice in a row.
On me these days I want only
breeze and brim.
Soft sweater, linen pants, hat
of woven straw.
Calm colors to neutral
my way out.
Pockets full, but room
for one more key.

ACKNOWLEDGMENTS

Thank you to the publications below for first publishing versions of these poems.

Door Is A Jar: "The Volcanologist"

DMQ Review: "Woman Becoming Winston Churchill"

Gyroscope Review: "Trying On," "Midnights, Midlife"

The Halcyone: "The Witch Explains Herself to Snow White"

Maudlin House: "Two Million Sit-ups Later"

Midnight Chem: "Gray-Haired Sylvia Plath"

MiGoZine: "What Daughters Wear to Fly"

Molecule: "Wide Leg Pants"

Passengers Journal: "Skip the Scarf"

Ploughshares: "Standoffish"

Poets Reading the News: "Crop Top"

Postcard Poems and Prose Magazine: "Pelage"

Rat's Ass Review: "My Husband Asks Me If I Ever Think About Ronald Reagan," "My Mother Eating Onion Dip"

Rise Up Review: "Everything About My Broken Wrist Is Privileged"

Rogue Agent: "Therapy of Red Vines™"

Salamander: "The Dog Wakes Me Up in the Middle of the Night"

Stories on Stage: "My Closet"

SWWIM: "Cross Body," "Self-Portrait as Anne Sexton's Typewriter"

Westwind: "Diagnosis with Composite Organism"

THANKS

Thanks to those who let me unravel,
and those who inspired me
to sew myself back together again.

ABOUT THE AUTHOR

Hilary King was born and raised in Roanoke, Virginia. After spending over twenty years in Atlanta, she moved with her family to the San Francisco Bay Area of California. Her poems have appeared in *Ploughshares*, *TAB*, *Salamander*, *MER*, *Fourth River*, *SWIMM*, and other publications. Also a playwright, she is the author of the book of poems, *The Maid's Car*. She lives with her husband, dog, and two cats. She loves hiking and ribbon.

ABOUT THE PRESS

Riot in Your Throat is an independent press that
publishes fierce, feminist poetry.

Support independent authors, artists, and presses.

Visit us online:
www.riotinyourthroat.com

RIOT IN YOUR THROAT BOOKS

Sarah Beddow   *Dispatches from Frontier Schools*
Kathryn Bratt-Pfotenhauer   *Bad Animal*
Kimberly Casey   *Where the Water Begins*
Sonia Greenfield   *All Possible Histories*
Brett Elizabeth Jenkins   *Brilliant Little Body*
Melissa Fite Johnson   *Green*
Melissa Fite Johnson   *Midlife Abecedarian*
Hilary King   *Stitched on Me*
Courtney LeBlanc   *Exquisite Bloody, Beating Heart*
Shilo Niziolek   *Little Deaths*
Laura Passin   *Borrowing Your Body*
Sara Quinn Rivara   *Little Beast*
Laurie Rachkus Uttich   *Somewhere, a Woman Lowers the Hem of Her Skirt*
Karen J Weyant   *Avoiding the Rapture*

www.ingramcontent.com/pod-product-compliance
Lightning Source LLC
Chambersburg PA
CBHW030515130626
46549CB00007B/3004